T0070200

Poems of

The Void

Sreekanth Kopuri

PARTRIDGE

Copyright © 2019 by Sreekanth Kopuri.

ISBN: Softcover   978-1-5437-5240-3
           eBook   978-1-5437-5241-0

All rights reserved. No part of this book may be used or reproduced by any means, graphic, electronic, or mechanical, including photocopying, recording, taping or by any information storage retrieval system without the written permission of the author except in the case of brief quotations embodied in critical articles and reviews.

Because of the dynamic nature of the Internet, any web addresses or links contained in this book may have changed since publication and may no longer be valid. The views expressed in this work are solely those of the author and do not necessarily reflect the views of the publisher, and the publisher hereby disclaims any responsibility for them.

Print information available on the last page.

To order additional copies of this book, contact
Toll Free 800 101 2657 (Singapore)
Toll Free 1 800 81 7340 (Malaysia)
orders.singapore@partridgepublishing.com

www.partridgepublishing.com/singapore

For **Jayanta Mahapatra** and **Runu Mahapatra**
who were the meanings of many silences

Deep in the forest there's an unexpected
clearing that can be reached only by someone
who has lost his way.

Tomas Transtromer, "The Clearing"

Darkness falls. At midnight I go to bed.
The smaller boat sets out from the larger boat
You are alone on the water.
Society's dark hull drifts further and further away.

Tomas Transtromer, "Under Pressure"

Acknowledgements

My greatest debt is to Jayanta Mahapatra who taught me the difference between poetry and sentimental scribbles two decades ago when we first met at his home. This still wobbly but sincere beginning would not have been possible without his intimacy which I must also attribute to my maiden research presentation on his poetry at the University of Oxford and many subsequent ones. *The Void* would be void without his continuous encouragement.

I am ever grateful to Ricardo Pau-Llosa the Cuban-American poet and art critic for his long discourse mails with his detailed comments on my poems, his valuable time and for chiselling out the excesses by doing some. Especially they have disciplined my jittery hand with sincere efforts for consistency in rhythm and density of metaphor. It was his prompt and quick response from time to time that helped me to grip my pen tight.

It is really a great honour to have most valuable comments and suggestions on a few of my poems from Burt Kimmelman, an American poet. It was most memorable experience to learn the remarkable difference between a complete and an incomplete poem and to sieve the inadvertent fill ups. There were a few poems which were rejected but were published in some journals when I abided by his valuable corrections particularly in carefully filtering the imagery to titles' relevance.

I am emotionally ever indebted to my brother Sanjai babu, who is an ideal of my parents in love and responsibility with his prayers and guidance, and for always being behind my consistency in thinking about life.

And above all, my poor words are too inadequate to thank 'The Word', that is the meaning of my birth, my death and my destination and which loved me more with its life.

A number of poems in this book first appeared in various journals / magazines / newspapers and anthologies in USA, Canada, Philippines and India to which the author gratefully acknowledges permission to reprint:

"My Shoe's,Letter," *Wordfountain,* Wilkes Barrie, USA

"Taj Mahal", "Kites", "Mimosa", "Dawn" *Ann Arbor Review,* Ann Arbor, USA

"Time", *The Paragon Journal (Omnistoria),* Pennsylvania, USA

"An Absence", *Foliate Oak Literary Magazine,* Arkansas, USA

"A Defeat", *Oddball Magazine,* Massachusetts, USA

"A Futile Legacy", *Ariel Chart Magazine,* North Carolina, USA

"Tsunami December 26th 2004", "Parting", "Communion" *Scryptic Magazine,* Detroit, USA

"Rain Again", "On an Old Photograph" *Forty Eight Review,* California USA

'Words', *Five 2 One Magazine,* California, USA

"To a Demented Professor" *Missing Persons: reflections on dementia,* (anthology) Beatlick Press. Albuquerque, New Mexico, USA

"Solitude", *A Flood of Contentment: Past of Letters, A Soul Series,* (anthology) The International Library of Poetry, Huddleston. USA

"The Autumn Hues of India", *Halcyondays Magazine,* Ontario. Canada

"Death of Solitude", "Fragments of Time" *The McKinley Review,* Manila, Philippines

"Seeking Meanings", "Shams" *Vayava,* New Delhi, India.

"A Soldier's Wife", *Indian Periodical,* August, New Delhi, India

"The Word", "To an Existentialist", "For a Reformer", *Poetcrit:,* Shimla, India

"Relationship", "'Its President Obama", "From Turmoil to Bliss", "A Memory", "A Voice of Foetus", *Indian Research Journal of Literatures in English,* Madurai, India

"Asylum", "The Flower of Liberty", "Promise of Joy", "Nature My Teacher" *Deccan Chronicle*, Hyderabad, India.

Contents

On an Old Photograph

A time frame hangs me
between the known and the unknown
beyond the glass
stilled by words
a grey souvenir bigger than the earth,
sometimes it is a train's window pane,
images pass the eye
blinded by time.

We are like the line of holes
on a flute's dark wooden face.

Words

I dip the line of thought
to fish out a word.

Some are on the surface
and some deep inside
all circling round the line.

Somewhere one stimulates
the hand of the thought.

It takes home a salmon.

To Jean-Paul Sartre

The words of pain could
rise only above turning
down an earthly honour.

Seventy five years of an
existential darkness sleeps
in a dilapidated tomb

but still the beatitude
of a meanest flower
and noontides give the
testimony of a shoulder
that hasn't shrugged off
the atlas and its pain.

Behold the footprints on the
splinters of a blurred glass
beyond the Whitmanisque
multitudes where The Word
builds life from the melted
clocks, dust and ashes.

Marxism

Left in the vision behind
the broken eyeglasses,
the epitomised tools of labour
age and rest in a cosy embrace
with the blunt edged desire.

Here an engineer turned "Marxist"
holds a blunderous biography
re-shuffling the crumpled pages
of violence that do not fail to echo
their terminal voice

that recedes into the clarion call
of the crucified 'silence's love,
the edge of its nails dripping with
the crimson life, already suffused
into the burnt out voice that shines
only as a golden epitaph in the
London Highgate Cemetery.

Between the Genesis of life and
Revelation of the truth termites are
born to live on the flesh that held
the guns of history and built the
ephemeral libraries that carry the
legacy of time-bound revolutions.

Today a handful of labour unionists
gather before the Machilipatnam
police station to organise a humble
leftist rally that ends with the alcoholic
puffs out of the slumber in the police van.

To a Demented Professor

(to late Prof. Sasthri of Bapatla Engineering College)

"Professor of computer engineering or…"
he introduces himself to a handful of humans,
trying to shoo away a pair of bitches playfully
snarling over a ragged slipper at the college gates.

Those stately constructions of a
so-called communal strength and
an elemental glow in a granite attire
are deceptive adornments of beauty

some nostalgic wounds, mock him
but are "only like a fragment
in the scrap heap beside my bed
unwanted as myself" he mocks.

A flock of pigeons explode the
hope of a reappointment into a
great flutter nostalgically echoing
in the department of civil engineering

but deaf-eared to his gabbles
about some blues of deprivation,
while he asks for a rupee or two.
Does that annoy? A pity!

On the last visit to ours invited me home
and Proclaimed: "There was a time dear boy
I was revered for mobilizing funds.
They owe a lot for my yeoman's service",

suddenly rummaged through crumpled dailies,
leaned on me saying, "You should be a sub-editor
boy for *Bharat-Bhoomi* - My dream magazine. I will
scandalize those notorious landlords (*chaudaris*).

A curtain of twilight counts
the autumn years of senility
shading the halo of knowledge
and the slippers bears his cross.

"Great delegates will throng to my funeral
with heavy hearts and news paper profiles
on me will shame my students." Went on....
oblivious of the half-sipped tea of life.

A post-waiting-for-Godot existentialist?
An unlucky Pozo or Lucky?
A manifestation of identity in an irredeemable exile?
Suddenly clouds swarm and vanish

taking away the elemental hope from him
leaving only a storm in his half sipped teacup
An embarrassed Mrs.Shastri avoids visitors.
Occasionally a train hoots a presage of some death.

Hope

We die
like great trees
but the roots of
memories hold
deep into the earth
that waits for the
fresh monsoons
of our dreams
to sprout some
hopes around.

India

When the rain-drenched
old wooden face of the
bullock cart's wheel that's
sunk in the mud of the
Pedana fields, and Karna
shoulders the ancient burden
of its epic strains with his
face at the mobile towers,
the Sun's signals swing his
golden earrings enlightening
him towards a red, rusting
tractor that is yet to trace
the tracks towards a combine
for a golden harvest.

Karna: A major character in the Indian Epic
Mahabarata.

After the Ashes

I can live now but not
without the broken bread
and bleeding vine
beyond the womb
and the half,
clock and sands,
and the coffin of
the Hammer and Sickle.

Now dreams explode into
a white bonfire, flutter
with the strength of humility

to nest in that love that
encloses me with thorns
that hallow a death,

open the eyes of secret silences
of time that stood against
earth's celebrated mausoleums.

The darkness that trickles down my eyes
today in sack-cloth as milk can curdle
the honey of that perennial venom.

From the wild grass at the feet of
the *Angel of grief* Rome, a cluster
of life humbly waits for the sun.

Michelangelo's Adam

(After Visiting the Sistine Chapel, Rome)

He is born again
in Rome instead –
a new testament
between the heaven
and the earth.

It's good for the man
to be alone on the earth –
paradise lost and
the earth regained

for the woman too
but in heaven –
the earth lost and
paradise regained

eve-teasing Adam
teasing eve
from the earth,

and Adam-teasing eve
teasing Adam
from the heaven.

A Day at Auschwitz

(after visiting the Auschwitz concentration camp, Poland)

A bleak sunless morning
would be right to know the

meaning of death and meaning's
own. The wheels of Krakow bus

are burdened with our curiosity,
stagger and screech to halt at the

"Museum Auschwitz" stop
at last. The ash flakes of

my long soaked dream spill
down on the rusty gates of

The Shame open for the
visitors today, showcasing

the tatters of six million silences
disgorging streams of visitors

like the omens coming alive
from the skulled memories of

the dead innocence' lost dreams.
This is what we are dressed in

our Sunday best for, on a picnic-
spree, making a line of humans

to know the synonyms of a naked
truth of those cattle-lines, saunter

through the arched promise –
arbeit mecht frei, on a terminal

earth's long crumpled scroll of
roll calls into a silence occasionally

broken by the invisible chirrups
from the sentient chestnut trees along

into the cold sooty furnaces gaped
open with the weight of a million

absences, displaying *Men in
Striped Pyjamas* who live hanged

in portraits on blackened white-
washed walls of the Aryan pride

engraved *a race that must be totally
exterminated –Hans Frank 1944.*

My cam trespasses to steal the preserved
vengeance in those blinded spectacles,

shaving brushes, prayer mats. shoes,
children's clothes, dolls and a seven

thousand dark coiled remains of its fury
– the fleeces, showcased in the frozen

eyeballs of history, only a fraction of
a hatred's weight. A fourth generation

visitor breaks down at the sight of the
preserved hair when an usher reminds us

silence. My footprints sign a testimony
on the ashes of this graveyard of leftovers

of an apocalyptic trial – a failed
succession of a delusive visionary.

Machilipatnam

History's spilled leaf soaked
beneath the mossy stones of
time's cornered light, scents
of the English and the French –

the squares of my domicile's
identity, prides in this sweet
amber earth – *Bandar Laddu*
– that rotates its Telugu flavour,

proclaimed by Krishna's mouth of
the Bay of Bengal and the rhythmic
melody of kuchipudi steps that the
grey haired brush of Kalamkari art

paints in the farm fresh fruit colours
shining as the Chilakalapudi rold
gold that smiles bright like the
morning sun at Manginipudi beach,

the proud tricolour of a forgotten
patriot's hand humbly shoulders the
Cambridge of South India slowly
losing its traces in the trajectory of

time. A fragrance of another evensong
from an ancient mausoleum's pulpit of
St Mary's Church flits across the Koneru
Center's fountain eye that jets a moist

silence into its stilled clocks of our
deserted memory. We are boats,
anchored to the promised port still
roped to government's greasy palms.

Notes: Noble College which is one of the oldest
colleges in India was established in 1843 is popularly
called "The Cambridge of south India."

Bandar Laddu: A famous Indian sweet originated
from Machilipatnam

Kalamkari: A hand-painted cotton textile from
pedana

The Void

When the apple tempted
my mother's desire, the

answer slithered with a
knowledge as vengeance

and exploded *the Big Bang*
that severed the cord in the

navel beyond. Here a birth
cries in death's cradle now

suckled black milk by the
breast of a vengeance that's

sown in the elemental veins
and the pride of nations. It

explodes a centrifugal order.
Maggots deployed still search

life under the burnt chambers
of Auschwitz and the Syrian

debris. Our naturally black
marrow skins the earth that

burns the terminal morrows
of the dying flicker in the

wind of time. The sun sweats
into the dark blue moon. The

bones of a lion and the tender
petals of a wilted rose are worn

by the sharp edge of the time's
brandished smile. When the

waters of our learning trespass
with the quest of earthquake in

the trenches of determination,
graveyards are adorned by the

spiders and ants for the coronation
of a revenge against The Word that

bleeds under the pervading
shadows of the void. The

hoof-beats of the nations' pride sink
in the sands of the earth's judgement.

Grief

a tear runs down
the earth's eye

a sandpiper tethers along
these sandy dunes of
a prolonged absence

here a half sunk boat
dilapidated by broken dreams
stinks of dead fish

birds winter again
and the silence of desire
worms the blood
before the soul's last flight
to the bleeding Sun

Seeking Meanings

We are always too late,
before the worst breaks out
like a midnight storm, because
the secrets of the dynamics lie elsewhere
beyond our clouded conscience.

Today my mother sits alone
in my father's room
and breaks down for answers
unlike the scattered shadows
of the morning light
that stretches slowly into night
when the birds are back
into the nests like answers
to the daylong cries of their fledglings.

We look *deep into nature*
to *understand everything*
but the meanings and the words
are still our own;
they draw us back into our narrow selves
till all the golden mornings of life
turn into the russet haze of the last evening.

The Last Birthday of My Father in the ICU, CMC, Vellore

pain balloons
burns,
like a candle flame

his lips flicker
and trickle a prayer
down the eyes

silent last birthday rose
needling like a thorn in his
sagged balloon-like flesh
caked with a culture
in his temple

a geriatric
ward, off
like in isolation
in senility

a mobile of
unanswered calls

sad smile
in the sun's face
fading away
like evening light
a last wish

PS: Happy journey Dad, See you there

Jayanta Mahapatra

A Science becomes a poem
lost and found in the letters
of the earth's lyrical voices.

A silence in a broken heart
of dual faiths louder in its
humble dignity. A gray

absence brighter than a vast
presence in the light of the
luminescent black pagoda.

A petrichor of rain on the
earth of a muted identity,
spreading its fragrance into

the golden leaves of the
nation's pride. A redeeming
war of peace against the

Ashokan edicts with a handful
of "artless brown flowers"
offered at the ruined altar

of the glorious Kalinga. A
"Hunger" with the envious
tongues of flame burning inside

the belly of an earth that will
stretch its fragrant sands of love
as a feather-bedded tomb where

he dreams to sign off, leaving
behind a vast foliage of untold
saga. The smile and the grief

too, on the parched lips of the
Chandrabhaga where the ripples
of it's music, leave behind .a

trajectory of his signatures
stretching beyond the periphery.
A human wheel of the lord

Jagannatha's chariot, shouldering
the burden of a ravaged history,
breaking down to the earth in the

odyssey of a *Relationship* drenched
in a perpetual stream of blood in the
heart of a nation proclaiming its identity,

in the elevated glory of Konarka. A
turbulence from the "hidden springs
of *Mahanadi*", meandering into the

timeless waters of elemental eternity
becoming a sublime prayer from the
slit throats of the Sun god's children.

Voice of a Foetus

I'm the ripening fruit
of desire in you.

I know I'm not the sun
that will rise above the mountains

of your hope tomorrow but you know
there are hands in the world that wait for me.

Life isn't in the garbage heaps
nor in a pack of stray dogs.

My unknown fathers disown me.
So, let me cry a cry of hope
before it recedes into silence.

The Unfair Drafts

The morning drafts are
always unfair unlike
the simple flower.

The day is long along the
wide avenue that sans a
beginning and an end
for the times pace up
and down beyond the
human science.

A pastor's cry
at the London pulpit
will only recede
far behind his daughter's
clarion call among
the rocky terrains of
the aging guerrillas.

Today you are lost
somewhere at the war
between love and weapons
amidst the fallen pigeons to
find the serpentine secrets
in the womb of Eden.

The Taj Mahal

Words lose their way
like the dry leaves and suffuse
into the grandeur of a mausoleum
where art recites the history
of a love's lyrical madness

a death becomes a broken dream,
a grand loneliness towers
in the splendour of minars
beyond the range of an artist's eye
with the fossilized epic that
runs along the eloquent marbles
in the wild silence of alien letters

and the timeless moonlight
resorts to the empty nuptial nights
beside the perennial waters
of an emperor's lost voice.

An Unfinished Journey

(A homage to Dr YS Rajasekhar Reddy)

It's too late before the state became India's
beckon light on the global threshold,

before your fate was visible on the face of the
Pavurala Gutta (pigeon hill), breaking

the silence of peace you wove in the brittle nests
of the mud-folk, humbling their pride of you.

The clocks of Andhra Pradesh make centripetal
strains towards that golden beginning.

A wisp of smoke goes up in haste from the
dark wick of a candle lit in a patient hand

trailing 500 souls along the footprints
of the state's redefined history.

A persecuting crack in the triune state of the
arrested cords of an assassinated heart.

A dark wind flickers the restless *white cards* of hope
in the thatched confines of the hungry.

A little boy sits on the steps of Machilipatnam's
St. Andrews Church to read Mathew 10:8

when a 108 wails somewhere half way along
the road not yet taken to that dream

drenched in the dried eyes of a heart that still pounds
your name in the slit wrists of a bleak future.

White cards: Also called white ration cards are the
Identity cards for the people who fall below poverty
line in Andhra Pradesh

My Shoe's Letter

Dear Sir!
This is your old companion
from the garbage heap.

I remember biting
your hasty foot
at first acquaintance,
reminding the
mutual adaptability
along the *miles to go*

age with you
into every sunrise
as strong soul mate
born to guard your foot
as a white-hearted angel,

your dairy to preserve
miles of memory
in a sleepless howl
of burdensome silences

you scuffed my soul
many a time, yet I bore
those injuries to feed with
the lessons for another journey
into the unknown and the
cobbler too beside the road
of potholed dreams
with his day's bread,

while in rest, I pray,
and swallow all your fears
with my huge mouth of
toothless gums, with a
classic grip stronger
than an alligator's,

lately when you tried
a new road of
un-treaded cobblestones
I held gently as a
lion holds its cub.

PS: Kindly excuse this
letter, tattered as my
telltale skin.

———————❂———————

A Futile Legacy

(for an un-English mother in dangerous dreams)

Can you paint yourself red fond of English?
or dare walk into these Indian streets
in a perfect English attire?

Can you speak English English?

Can a language however resplendent and glorious
substitute the language of heart
and the voice of your ancestors?

Isn't the mother-tongue of the *Jaravas* of the
Andamans
as good to them as English to the English?
or Telugu to the Andhras?

Like a mighty banyan struggling to uproot itself
in a bid to reach the sky
you carry your own offspring
towards some unreachable horizons
of a great language
where
I'm afraid
these poor children
will beg one day
for a mother-tongue
on some barren lands of alienation
or somewhere in the furrows
between humans and animals
and be a bunch of ridicule.

Isn't this like forcing them
to live in space without a foothold?

Isn't this a dangerous legacy
which once again originates
in a root cause of uprooting of civilizations?

Won't they miss the essence of life
and some divine missions?

Do you not feel that you need
a bed of your mother-tongue
to dream of an alien language?

A gift of one hundred tongues
needs a linguistic shelter of your own.

Let them not be victims of your pride and vanity.

It isn't too late mother!
Open your eyes before they speak-
these poor kids-
a language patched with Dravidian fragments of
English.

A Defeat

Shadows shift back and forth
a man's face disappears into his wife's
and appears to her again in her friend's.

A yellow leaf of conscience trembles
on the edge of a resolution.

A rain of clouds washes away
a long dream scribbled
on the sprawling sands of
a melting clock.

A flock of gulls explode
into a terrible absence.

An old jasmine fragrance tries again
to widen the spaces between
the rock of ages and the aging boat
of a mortal wound.

Soft-wearing

How weary stale, flat and unprofitable
seem to me all the uses of this world
-   Hamlet

We are chips
chipped off
discs of
transmigrated souls
less in the weight of love.

"What's up?" asks
my grandmother.
"Whatsapp" i say.
That's all we live for.

A new learning puts us
at a dangerous ease
crushing the dreams
of life under heavy
digital missions of mind
in the gullies of the
metropolitan trash cans.

Brains drain out
in the confluence
of brain drain.

Miles away the soil
moans with pain
where the womb
of love travels
the road that leads
to the larger rooms
of senility where even
lovemaking is digitalised.

Ganesh Ritual

Sridevi wraps the graceful folds
of autumn's rippling smile around
her golden texture, in saffron sari,
an offering to the dark naked clay
Ganesha, the autumn-born belly
god, marks the seasonal sanctity
at the door, steps into the lush
guava orchard, plucks the ripe
dreams smiling green on the
Ganseh chaturthi pandal that
bears the season's mellowing
hope in the parrot-green elephant
apples and the incense wisps of
her burning piety with a mousy
humility, around which the radiant
circles of her devout hope halo
the natural wisdom that the earth
gives as the four-armed elephantine
providence of the creation.

Shams

It's all
what the leaves of the earth rustle about.

A blade of grass in the graveyard
cuts the elusive wind
which opens no secrets of its destination

nor the distances beyond the known
the eye of a flower soars
nor of its fading smile.

When the aging horses of the human blood
pace the time,
meanings disappear
in the clouds of dust
like their voices
in the hoof beats.

When a tribal girl aborts
to save the guilt of some men
who feed her,
and when a faith calls her an adulteress
can one still offer his cheek
for another slap?

Today it's calcium carbide
that ripens the fruits
and wax that glistens them
and life's ant-line search on the hidden meanings.

Independent India

The long freedom's hunger
slithers into the decomposed
heaps of tranquillity, for a bite

or two to inject the unity of
the wiping strength in the
sacred fangs of the fanatic

belief in the tricoloured fold
of a maturing diversity where
politics is wedded to religion

before the holy fire of a non-
violent history. A lost beggar
counts his hard earned alms

of freedom on the pavement
of the potholed national highway
that bears the government convoy

which invests an amicable smile
of saccharine electoral promises
for another flickering victory of

empty pages hard bound to bear the
scribbled ideas that will jam again
at the empty ATMs, and death of

the only bread winners of the poor.
In mercy's untouchable can of excreta
that hangs down her helping hand

is the real burden of untouchability
stinking with the *pride and prejudice*
of a faith's mounting aberration that

sets the constitutional order which the
the *Ashoka Chakra* spins on the unfurling
colours of prosperity and peace our saluting

hands of mere independence day patriotism
are innocent of for that frozen conscience
naturally repels the light of democracy.

Does the lionized emblem on the *Adhar Cards*
rewrite our fate ensuring the ration to the
thatched shadows in Machilipatnam slums?

Another august handful of peace explodes
in a minister's hand as a ritual of freedom
while the battalion of nation's pride marches

off another year into a new beginning,
with the unchanged garments of self-
justice, "of, for and by the people."

Honour Killing

(*in the memory of Pranay*)

"Honour's" daughter wedded
"dishonour's" son,

conceived innocence and
dishonoured "honour"

who buys a crore of revenge
slits the throat of

a young dream that groans with the
premature labour pain

yielding to the primitive strength
of a prejudice' faithful hatchet

soaked in the pool of a muted
voice on this *Good Earth*,

the Hindu-Christian cord of which is severed
by the scalpel of a Muslim conspiracy.

The sun sets down the grave darkness
drenched in the dirge

- *ashes to ashes* - of love's bleary eye and
the honour's trickling question's

some questionable answers in the mutually
pricking communal kingpins

in the nation's best television debates,
end in smoke of

the endless storm in their
emptied tea cups

that wail *Love's Labour's Lost* –
a mere silence

spilled at the rooted feet of
"the honour's" green pride.

Kites

Because this window bars
the world and the dreams age
with every dawn drying up
the salt in the eyes, today
the hands try a kite of
silent words red and blue that
the spool unravels into a silence
where they want to break down
to the last syllable that:
"this life is a false start so let me
chirrup a song of new joy
in the vast world of a little nest
somewhere" but at the sun down
the darkness reminds
we are the kites of the earth
let off only with a dirge of time.

Asylum

The board read:
the visitors those who
come here to watch them
for the sake of pleasure
are punishable.

An ugly spot on the cheek
of the charming city
abandoned and awaiting pity.

a big city beside the coast
where the traffic is so vast

a natural city at Bengal's coast
wishes to be the world's host

my mind urged to here last night tomorrow
not yet decided for its full of sorrow

a guard I saw at its gate
who responded to receive me late

suspected for I expressed innocence
and said going in is nonsense

the asylum isn't for an entertainment
but sincerely for an improvement

a mile between their cells and the gate
for such is their fate

with helpless thoughts starts their dawn
with senseless doubts do they yawn

everyone's away from home
with no way to roam

they eat but after many hours
when the nurse's approach mentally nears

to their past senses they hardly come back
as their psyche is on a wrong track

they knew not the sense of being homesick
for their brain matter is so weak

so alarmingly did I waver in that mad world
and for long haunted by the sad world
men of all ages
unshaved like sages

the grace in their faces faded
the furrows under eyes shadowed

God's in his heaven
Millionaire in his bhavan
Madman's but gloom-driven
All is wrong with this world

Passion of Our Earth

When the burning flames
of our watery heart's hornet swarms

around its ravaged nest, the
silent, strange breeze touches its

glassy eyes. It's splinters
spill an intuition about the wavelength

of our moist soul.
We are still here in the thistly grip

of the perpetual circles crowned
around the head of the crucified earth.

The tireless carpenter ants
that crawl into the crevices of the old pine

still emit the fragrance
of the long dead pigeon's burnt flesh.

The spilled feathers
that carry the truth still move

the wind's direction,
guided towards their fixed destination.

The Brief Candle of Andhra

Icy silence
celebrates its first birthday
without a cake of hope to stand on.

Today it sings a Telugu song
with a flaming tongue
amidst the sad gladiators
left behind by an Italian dream
that disappears into its colosseum.

Now the song of the brief candle
struts and frets
only to end in smoke.

It melts down to Earth
as April crosses this crucified history.

The Burden of the Earth's Cross

Many drowned in silence
blinded in the cataracts of
the earth's aging eyes

the fallen sound passes away
across its waxed ears
today many golden ones

hanged in its neck
reflects its light
but drawn into its sands

raised above the hardened
lime-washed memories
of bone-white voids feeding
the wriggling white hungers.

The Autumn Hues of India

The heat of Indian summer
put down to the earth's magic
spell on the stretching bed of
the autumn foliage, under the
ripeness of the old mango tree
of my home where the mynas
do not complain against the
gathering crows and the turmeric
-yellow Asian hornets, for it is
time to learn from the ripeness
of the fallen leaves where the
golden oriole hops on the russet
stretches of evening for *ripeness
is all*, searching the meanings of
winter's bleakness with the
camouflaged wheatish mantis
joining hands, becoming the
atoms of the unfading life's
heaped orange windfalls on the
honey bee-swarming pushcarts
along the red-soiled beauty of the
Machilipatnam streets, signing *India*.

A Passage

The aging solitude
a heap of bones
wrapped around
a sagging costume

strolls along
the wayward way
of these sandy dunes

towards the hands of
that enigmatic clock
beyond where the feet
search the oasis of meanings

waits with the hollowed eyes
for the grandeur
of that last ceremony.

Fragments of Time

A crow-call cracks
the stony silence of
the blurred glass face
of the enigmatic clock,
its broken hands scattered
around like the *apple, ball*
on my niece' broken slate.
Memory's weak fingers
leaf through some crumpled
moments in the deafening
silence of this room when
someone suddenly stamps
crackling their leaves among
the greying marbles where
long absences blur the words
of life's dusty ruined epitaphs.

The Defiled Friday

(in the memory of the victims of the Hyderabad Mecca Masjid Bomb Blast)

An indignant old crow stains
the Charminar's splendorous minaret

and a swarm of flies disappear
as the mango slices suddenly turn bitter

in the hands of the street children.
The innocent water washes some feet

near a volcano that sleeps
in a masjid's lunch box and suddenly

in some hundred flutters of innocence
is peace ruffled into the mid-summer sky

that remains silent to the cries of
the Friday defiled by splashes of red, painting

a lasting picture on the
obsolete canvass of Gandhian endurance.

An odyssey of years comes
to a staggering halt where every snarl-up

at the major squares is
scared stiff of this age old game.

The cynical barrels of
the government bang at the riotous frenzy.

The water cannons wash away
only the summer dust at the feet of Charminar.

The tired day disrobes its stained garment,
and a gust of some mysterious wind hisses and

slithers to patrol these
deserted streets under the silver cascades.

Defiled Saturday

(in the memory of the victims of Lumbini Park & Gokul Chat Bomb Blasts)

A notorious adventure
triumphs over us, off its grip

life gropes its
stuttering fingers elsewhere.

Once again a familiar panic
spiders from a defiled Friday to

those celebrated spots
of a city's pride and redefines the life

heedless to the call
of that something called truth or love.

Gokul and *Lumbini* are but
mangled remains, dislocated hands of time

pass an irrational legacy
to the ends of the nation and beyond.

Readily the television
calls us to identify some half nude torsos

in the safety of
the government morgues.

Some earthworms in
the cosy womb of the earth

or cockroaches
in the crevices of a rock

or beetles in the
stinking layers of a dung heap

or even pigs
wallowing in the slush

would've been safer
for their deaths have a special providence.

We've become
dangerously contented with our own safety.

Feelings start to die in
the stoic fold of our blood and

we still go in grand processions to
dip the lifeless idols in contaminated waters,

slash out blood on
the soulless hearts of heroism

in street rituals
in the painful memory of a great escape

a mutual provocation
for another history till again somewhere

some tiny tots
do not return home.

Paper Boats

dreams spilled
down to earth
from the truth but
carry their own
dream scripts
that blot out in the
truth's endless streams
unfolding the truth that
the earth returns us
to its verdict

Pebbles of the Sea

words of time
soaked in the
noontides of
the elemental
sermons of truth
holding the earth's
account in the
movements of its
insomniac hands

The Dying Lepers

While silence blinks the night's
eye, emptying the light from
the blinded lamps of the lepers'

thatched hope, scurrying in
and out of the garbage heaps
with mouthfuls for a rainy day,

the leprous goldsmith searches
his face in the sooty mirror of
broken future, and evasively asks

his wife once again, *should I still
wait or leave?* A reply hangs down
her eye, tosses and creaks on the

telltale charpoy, counting the terminal
throbs of the invisible wooden-faced
clock in her blood, presaging

the end of a goldsmith's generation.
Somewhere an elegy struggles
to break the suffocating shell,

egging on the enigmatic fate.
What lies beyond those worn
out clay Ganesha and portraits

of all those armed Gods? Perhaps,
the bloody vermilion that cracked
her head every day, the diffused

face of the gold flake king size
cigarette smoke and the truth
know. At least, the innocent

offerings of the coconut bowls,
and the skyward looking incense
sticks are fragrant and sweeter.

A familiar gush flickers the credit
of bank notes on the table, awaiting
a bottle of wine or a terminal journey

to his concubine in the HIV colony of
Bapatla, and the world beyond for the
flaming tongues of the ultimate communion.

Note: Traditional married women of India draw a
straight line with vermillion on the head along the
parting of hair as a symbol of sacredness.

Endurance

A silence sweats and rages
falling in words
crumpled into balls of paper.

Its home wears and
the walls start to peel.

A couple of doves sojourn
on the attic and vacate,
spilling some quills
of inked meanings.

Half-a-life's hands
pick them and
the scattered twigs
only for a memory.

The wind whispers
in this deafening ear
about the worm that
bulges in a ripening fruit
of a time-tested endurance.

Parting

The river parts
but the old sands are still wet

thoughts recede to you
like a lost butterfly

life unleafs into bone boles
birdless deflowered and leafless

still a lonely fruit hangs
like a last hope

the aging stone of life's eye
parching in this desert of sandstorms
waits for the return of an eternal monsoon.

Tsunami, December 26th 2004

(*in the memory of the victims in Machilipatnam*)

Tides and tremors write history
breaks the heart of the earth
into a natural graveyard along

the shore strands many,
who wait for death,
watch like a great audience

a hungry circle of land
gape open its mouth
wag tongues of flame

crunch scores of corpses
into a smouldering pile of ash
building a tomb of history

dogs stalk a naked babe of hope
that picks bread crumbs among ruins
to feed the future hope.

"Open your eyes please!
I'm here with you dear,
nothing will happen",

the boatman slaps his dying wife
shrieks mad, presses belly
to vomit the water and aerates

running random for help
fainting on her dead body
ending a tale of love

night falls silently in varied forms –
dogs eat a human corpse,
ravens drag away the intestines,

rats pickup bones to
preserve as hard memories, and
ants lick off its traces to build hills.

Can a thousand poems
or a million tears
or a million more sighs

undo the tragic loss,
bring back the departed souls,
pacify the elemental wrath?

Even a Santiago couldn't have
fought back this holocaust but
rewritten "man is made for defeat."

All the doctorates of seismology
and doctrines of technology
couldn't forecast this catastrophe

but animals could flee
to a safer place before
we could feel the tremors

What's man Tsunami
before your overnight judgement
of his dismal destiny?

Listen those helpless cries
reverberating along the ravages.
The waves still threaten

Come again saintly mother
from the city of palaces
kindle a divine lamp of hope.

In the twilight of the year
the enraged sea extended its steps
in a catastrophic dance,

leaving behind
only the skeletons
on the sands of time.

A Destination

Those bruises see
that the time's ashes
beneath these aging feet
will bring home a love
beyond all our meanings
but not yet, since the
ash flakes of these dreams
still blur the way.

The Soldier's Wife

She is wrapped in the purity of
a bone-white sari
forehead bare
hands disbangled

eyes emptied of sleep, darkened
with sooty half moons below
try a word with his unfading smile
hanged on the wall

a sea of despair trickles down
drenching the meanings of her past
and the hidden suns of the future.

The reminiscent voices of her lost soul
pound the breath of hope
suffocating the debris of
tragedy in the engulfing darkness,
where the hands of her deprivation
burry the last dawn
as the eternal sunset sets in.

Two kids!
one still at breast
the other at the kindergarten
haunted everyday with the question
"where's your dad?"
on the weekend parents' meet.

The government paltry sum, her bread,
body the space,
children the solace,
mirror the reflection of time
in the narrowness of sultry void.

The other day the nation
honoured her *Paramveerachakra*,
a perpetual barb of distinguished honour.

Fate's artful hand
drew her down
into a wary future.

Today he's a grand memory
a helmet-headed gun
on a tomb of his body and

she's a half drawn
distorted sketch of silence
abandoned by an invisible artist, who
contemplates an apocalyptic erasure.

An Illusion

the eye of talon
always haunts
the white innocence
leaping in the green
silence of the grass

perhaps a mystery that hangs
between the sky and the earth

may be the sea is always heavy
with the waves who always
struggle for a language for
meanings

the boats lie on the shore
like the bitten nails
of Rodin's absence

The Lost Tradition

Humanity slithers past
hungrily with its fangs

dripping hemotoxin of
fanaticism in search of

its prey while democracy
on its last journey to the

burning ghat drags its
wounded feet on the hot

sandy dunes of the deserted nation
lately the communal knife lanced

open the pregnant wombs of
different faiths and the alien

children molested to death in
the streets of mother's right hand

on its pool of blood
the red lotus rises in

the bliss of victory.
The live cremation

of the stainless missionary
with his two children stains

a great tradition today
and makes a great country

look small, crumbling its
stately honour to dust

on mother's left hand.
No longer is the nation

a sacred unravished bride
but an absurd fanaticism,

seduced pulling her hair runs
mad into the deserted streets.

Meanings

Often fleeting clouds of sly abstractions
themselves, alluring beyond words, awry

scary in tremors of our pursuit
bleary with our pulsating grief

often beckon the deer of our thirst
through the woods of perpetual exile

lest we be meanings ourselves driving ideas home
cycling and recycling hard only for the sands of time.

These wait for a canvass drenched in the needles
of time's rain with scarlet trickles, down to the earth:

a teen-bride waits for an unborn *Godot*
to undo the tatters of her aging motherhood

to peel off the skin of her wasted tears and
years that raised another from her womb,

a distraught youth offers his dead body on a cell tower
with
a note to the chief minister for the state's "special
status",

a son waits for a bed in an award-winning government
hospital
for his dying mother, for he doesn't have any "gifts"
for the staff,

a zealot of enraged devotees raze down a masjid
and another of a different faith, burn a train of priests

and when a convent is molested to conception
a blind faith compels the fruit of motherhood

all is fair in war against justice
silence against the wanton uproar.

but the smile on seasons' faces is
artless with their natural dynamics

united in elemental harmony – beatitudes
in unison, dressed in enigmatic nakedness

but with the fury of sudden calamities –
poetic truths against our crisp paper truths –

the ubiquitous meanings that we the leaves
of the earth, rustle about and fall as meanings.

Tea Folk

Another milk-white morning
pours into the town's tea-dusty

bazaar. Folk spilled here and there,
warming up in the endless melting

pots along the bazaars with pinches
of sugary granules at tea shacks with

spoonfuls of tea-dust-like guffaws
and giggles of the Indian brown faces

suffusing into the milky morning
boiling with the fragrance of native

exchange of pleasantries with the
warm sips of the cardamom tea.

Tomorrow

After the nuclear winter, when
the waters turn into its soot

a lost child walks alone shouldering
burnt violins to perform the earth's last rites

a lonely scorpion searches
for the bleeding love that can melt the stones,

it will be time the long secrets
will hold mirror to your heart and

the truth will break its silence among
the cries that will be the only grains of sand

so if you have a day to undo
the legacy of that primordial void

it will be perhaps when a lion
weans a lamb or an eagle a dove.

As the clock is still green
let the hands wreathe a rainbow

around this earth
to warn against our arms.

Transcendence

Death twitters towards a new shore
elsewhere, till the doors of a feather

-bedded solitude unlock into a white
blooming graveyard of stilled ancient

clocks where the euphonious lips of
sweet wilderness blow pipes of natural

meanings to aerate the skeletons back
to the antique cycle of the earth's grave

elliptical dynamics undoing the hidden
episodes of that *Big Bang*'s recurrent

circles to re-pick that handful of dust
with an unbroken ribcage for another

without the hungry apple tree and fig
leaves, to grow into a timeless vastness

of unknown revelation where our hand
will be a reflective mirror of ubiquitous

truth with eyes streaming only life even
into the marrows of death's vengeance.

Death of Solitude

That long sweet silence
is a mere stilled image of time

now in the hollowed eyes
of the black and white photographs

hanged on the white washed
walls, only an unseen echo voyaging

through the seasons, receding
with the lonely noontides in the habitual

embraces of a stranger's
coldness that burns in the dreams elsewhere.

In the brimming eyes of a
discarded calendar a smile waves me

from its empty pages
withdrawing into the unknown.

Death

Words slowly disappear
under intensive care.

We are the silent
syllables
that break down soon
into meanings,

after all dreams
disappear when the eyes
open
elsewhere.

(to my father, moments before his death
at CMC Hospital Vellore, 25th June 2014)

An Absence

The day starts.
The hands of
these doors
grope in vain.

It rains here and
a fallen leaf
rolls off searching
some traces in the
yesterday's sands.

A bird is nervous
in the nearby woods
at an unfavourable gush.

A crack in the
wholeness of this room.

The wind hesitates
to reach the table
and the chair sighs
with the burden
of emptiness.

Still some ants
Gather for
habitual tea stains.

A Lie

woven with the void of
years in the African sands,
borrowed from the
life's incomplete pages

sits in secure chair today
bought from the supermarket
as a highest bidder at a secret
government auction

the shallowness adorned in
showy kinesics entreats for scraps
of learning from another that
proclaims the biography of its own
blunder written with the stolen letters
from the pages of a ruined history

it picks up the leaves and windfalls
spilled under growing trees in the
government orchard with more lies
that socialize a life whose belly
bulges with the voracity for wealth

At the Visitors' Auschwitz

It is only the ashen gray the digital
pages preserve in our irrelevant eyes
now our learning fails to feel the

death pulse of this bone white earth,
tired of too many unknown footprints
frozen by the winters of time. When

we buy some meanings from a guide's
habitual extempore, the shame on the
stony faces of surrounding fence-posts

and their iron knotted questions prick
our numbed conscience, may be more
dead than death that our knees do not

know the sack cloth and ashes that may
bring the bones to life against the crisis
of meaning hardened as the dark blood

that still groans *stoj!* at our trespassed
cams eager to capture our proud smiles
unfeeling to the shrieking silences of the
ashy graveyard's pulsating heart beneath.

Mimosa

Would I have these words,
if you weren't a silence?

a handful of earth,
if you weren't a sprout of hope?

a rain of feelings,
if you hadn't a cluster of smiles
in the last evenings of my dying father?

There was a moment, suddenly
when some words
exploded in silence
out of the broken glassy window
of my eye, and
drew invisible lines.

At times I feel the keys
for a piece of an unheard music
to reach you filling the distances

and today the song of my heart
flits everyday like a lost butterfly
around the tender folds of your silence

till it becomes a muted epitaph
in the time's inexorable hands.

The Rain

My old father's sheep
at his half-grown rice fields
are trembled at
the first monsoon rain, but

not the ravenous crows of
my scare-crowed self
that must lead the flock
through the later rain but
holds a broken staff of life instead.

Distance

Sometimes when the
longing wind of impulses
is high on the hand till
it is nightfall and the

luminescent fireflies
in the blood search
for the words
circling around the
vast dark spaces
between the moments
in my diary

the distance between
the letters spreads
into a blank page
where the moments fall
in black and white
like the passing clouds.

The ash of time
then becomes a memory.

The Solitary Farmer

Between day and night
the solitary farmer ploughs
the land that scents with
the lost grains of yesterday.

The wetness of the impartial
rain knows where the land is
dried and the earth worms dead.

Time swarms like a flock of birds
around the furrows of the land.

A Burden

As a bubble bursts in silence
somewhere in my blood, the

veins of some dying violins
tighten to play their last voices

and my eyes softly wink back
the salt into its noontides

of melted clocks that wash
only some cracked shells

ashore on these sprawling
sands where the unseen

footprints of seasons ask
something the sky pours

down on the sea to burden
it with more stillness.

Rain Again

You are here
this late afternoon
with sweet windfall
under the guava tree
and the Earth's fragrance
of your first touch
to defeat my reason
into a child
with light feet
in your hands, but
the tremors of the grim history
you have buried
along the sands of my home
grip me like a startled child.

A Memory

(to Raghu)

When my eyes tired in search
of bread and spilled in the
furrows and dragged along
by the iron talons of the rich
ploughs in the grabbed land
of my brothers, and honour
jabbed by the ravens over the
cast(e) garbage heaped on the
head of Bapatla, you were
a meaning without words
my mother's presence in
this primitive wilderness.

A Dream

The doors slam me in
drench in salt of suffocation
that stinks of steel watches.
The eyes close and
a dream cracks the door
slams me out into a child
at the feet of a rainbow
who longs for a bone
of my ribs to mother
but the balloons
go off my hand.

Broken Dream

the clouds of two uncertain voyages
of eternity surround us again

a reunion in a rain of flowers under
this old bower of compromises

a bleakness haunts into an evening
of twitters without birds

a roar of waves without a sea
wraps me around you

a crack in your mountains of love where
the force of blood struggles

to spurt out the years of silence wandering
in the mortal corridors of absence

the fruit of pain and sweetness transforms us
into a birth of uncertain isolations

cart-wheeling along the stony road down
the mirages of endless streams

Another Rainy Morning

An hour more
and another morning
will unwind at my pillow
startle me out
of this dream
like a thunderbolt.

My neighbour's cow
will low out the day and
my hand will reach the pillow
for the snooze button.
The routine scribbles
and warm tea-sips
will try to draw out
the alluring fragments
of the last night's dream

and some tidings will be
emptied by the screens
and papers contesting
for the day's space.

A Wait

Night and day soak
in the watery eyes
of a child's dream.

Hope pulls its self
from heaps of stones;
while a thousand solitudes
smell of broken dreams.

A new morning explodes
with a million twitters
towards an unseen destination.

Time

My hands paddle
the lifeboat back
to the shores where
the lonely waves of
the lost joy trip it down
only to paddle back
again to the deep and
silent waters of another
uncertain morning.

Flight

When a grotesque reality of
forgiveness becomes the
question of life, then let the
life resort to pen to wander
on the paper of the earth and
from the cloudy sky of heart
and let the eyes rain the inky
blues to fill this perpetual void.

Communion

Dark ants swarm around
the bread of my home
its hands start to paralyze
looking down the earth where
the bones and ashes
wait for a reunion.

A wind
that has always been here
from my birth
ruffles the nest
of our questions, that
twitter off in vain
in their last flight.

In this tree of sublime silences
death holds the earth
for a purpose
in which we bury our lost faces
to understand.

An Answer

A stack of questions
we saunter towards you
who rest in the coffin
with balls of cotton in
nostrils as you cannot
bear the stink of life.

We are left behind
to become answers
for the bigger questions
that burden the Earth.

A Dawn

of sips and doors
a lost duckling
waddles into a terrible bleakness
under the drums of the sky

a scattered earthworm
drags its broken self
across the drenched road

a silent fledgling
in the dripping nest waits
for the unknown mother

the neighbour's cow lows
into this deafening silence
of painful absences which
creep into another dawn
nibbling at the edge

Good Friday

While the mid
summer afternoons pass
every year on the earth
like the leaves of
a stripped-down mango tree,

dust to dust and ashes
tell tales more
of the summers to come.

Easter

The Earth trembles
with awe at this
timeless solemnity
when the sepulchre's
message surpasses
the mechanics of $E = Mc^2$
as a testament of love
between the Earth
and the Heaven
time and eternity,
to unplague the
mortal history amidst
the fugue of elements.

The Flower of Liberty

The fully blossomed
flower of independence
already a quinquagenarian
as is vividly apparent in the
light of scientific advancement.

The corolla of human values
are withering and dropping
on the ground

The nation sky-rockets in science,
the rate of the downtrodden too
has increased with equal agility.
Amidst this the flower of independence
is only an object of decoration.

My hands unable to reach it
I want to water it
but my hands shackled
by rotten politics

I desire to hold the flower
but only the ugliness of
the battered constitution
crippled righteousness
and communal disharmony
is all that I come across.

Were the days before
August15th1947
any better than now?

As I thought this
a spark of inspiration
set ablaze in me
I want to take the flower
in my hands
But alas! I am fettered
What if there's no slavery? still
my hands though strong though
with unity in diversity and
multitudinous cultures
shackled with politicization

You know who am I?
My name is:
Of the people
For the people
And by the people

Can anybody redeem me?

A Novel Life

I see a bright face
with seraphic charm
rosy pink lips and
brimming youth

the inscrutable end of
a journey before her time
a divine message in silence

there! the soul
sleeping unruffled
on this flamboyant flower bed
the body embellished only for the soil
and the embalmed spices for stink
ready to move beneath six feet of earth
the gateway to the eternity

it's to here the soul makes
its unknown stately flight
beyond the mortal horizons
for a fresh start of a novel life

into the eternal abode
the sentiments
the worldly opulence
the earthly fame
it doesn't take
but leaves behind
only the shrieks of the
devastated loved ones and
attempts to console
its kith and kin in vain

alas! that soft milky face
shall only be food for worms

grave a fine and private place but none
I think embrace willingly.

Solitude

The parrot perched alone
on a branch embellished with leaves
fluttering in the gentle wind

drooping a gaze searchingly
for its missing mate
in the darkest hour of midnight.

The moon casts its fulgent flash
of silver gleam on it
to expose its beauty

but did anybody see its sorrow
its glossy eye welled with warm tears
and heart heavy for its missing mate?

Who knows the pain of its solitude,
its melancholic song,
the legendary grief,
and silent battles fought
in the unknown?

Will the missing mate
ever comeback?

When will his wait be over?

From Turmoil to Bliss

As usual, the barrels of
the city guns erect over the skyline,

emit clouds of smoke an
unseasonal downpour of ash flakes.

This keyboard strikes more
a note of isolation. The world appears

here on an empty square
of glass wall and after a while disappears

into my own sheepish reflection
but the arched smile of the exotic colours in

the tears of the sky descends
a promise - a song of swaying fronds.

The russet angel of twilight
rocks the cradle again, moments of life

into past in a kind of
domestic besidedness. A fish springs up

the pond and arches down
logging off the windows to a soulless world

while gleams of light
disentangle me from many webs in the

sites of tinsel knowledge.
Life's boat dances on the ripples of the river's smile.

Another Year

A while ago
the last gust left and
the boat brims with those
sweet fragrant nothings

two birds sit at the edge
and look into the tomorrow's sky
chirruping some promises of heart

a dream explodes
into a flight of birds
in sky of my heart

in the simple and
silent vastness of
this familiar landscape
a wish searches
for something deep

The Priest, His Wife
and the Young Girl

The soul of the girl is the subject, darling!
between you and me
like a swarm of flies
between a piece of cake
and my watering mouth of diabetes.

The conscience always ages
like woods where the deer
of desire is always lost
when the summer mirages
draw it like the midnight dreams.

It's another Sunday dear!
with the girl,
her distracting words,
and the roses of the youth
and the worm of desire
secretly wriggling
in the apple of this eye,

and The Word,
between us

with its question of the soul
like my walking stick
to walk the talk with her
along the dark, slithering road
towards our golden destination

but only with you
because....
this flesh is ailing
and I will be left behind.

———◦❋◦———

A Blind Night

The day nests into night's
feathery embrace where
sleep becomes a meaning for
another morning but silence
breaks the night's eye when

a highway bridge
collapses in Mumbai
into a sudden debris of funerals

the midnight bulletin of the
television suddenly announces
the cancellation of the 500 rupee note

a rickshaw-puller buys
some jasmines for his daughter's
nuptial where the hidden future
waits in silence like an eagle eye

blinding the vision of
the unborn morning that is
drenched with the weight of
the salt in the night's eye.

Woman

A Derrida
decentring
the sky
for the Earth with
her brain child
to conquer

A Pang

Desire burns alone
as the blood crackles
in tongues of flame
giving a meaning
to the ashes of
a broken promise
crushed between
two lives
and the voice of
their tears die
without the trace
of their time

Lost

The watery soul inside
the body's dark burnt
clay pot is alone on the
sands of the earth
where a raven quenches
its burning thirst on a
passionate midnight
tilting off the pot's emptiness

Time's dream is lost
while an angel shoulders
the sealed crowns to return
to the potter's bleeding hands
where this death awaits their touch
for the birth of a meaning
in a martyr's last breath
as a restitution.

A Letter to Bharata Ratna Dr. Br Ambedkar

Dear Baba Saheb!

When I went to
the Government Bank
in Amaravati yesterday,
to see my son "Joseph",
they said "none by such name"

but the watchman said
"your son is called Praveen
at his workplace, but
elsewhere on duty today."

I was grateful to his kind words
and glad that he meant his name
which means, "talent"
that was in the Government records.

Then I remembered your words,
If one converts to Christianity
he ceases to be an Indian

If my son disowns Christ
and calls it Democracy,
do I then have a right
to re-baptise and put his
Government job at stake?

In a dream that night
I saw a wall with
your name on it and
on its right the dreams of my son
were honoured at the feet of
the emblematic lions fluttering
on the national flag,

on its left a handful of "apostates"
were walking away
from *Chaitanya Bhoomi*
crossed by a pride of
hungry lions near the
oldest Buddhist monastery
in Hemis national park
on the India's head.

May be a Daniel
must come to judgement
for a dialogue between
the scheduled and
the unscheduled lives
of this *Good Earth*
for Christ's sake.

<u>From:</u>
Backward Community Candidate
C. Category (Indian Christian)

Redemption

Let these words fly out
of death's rib cage now
dear father!

because, only they
remain meanings
beyond the tombstone

live in death's crevices
of the Earth's conscience
a hand of truth to redeem it.

A Gift

My mother
gave me
a sackcloth
of ashes
to hide the
burnt coals
of my birth

A Pot

Humbled
down to earth

a dark lump
in the maker's hand

picked late
turned counter-clockwise

on the time's wheel
reshaped and burnt black

to hold more water
for the thirsty on the parched earth.

Blinded Vision

(after the accident on July 5ᵗʰ 2002)

This young eye
had many blank pages
waiting for
the dream-script
till the truth

a dream bigger than
the earth and death

a sea deeper enough
to drown the topless
clock towers but
while in a long
winkless wait to
reach the destination

a dark speck of
eye-quake from
the unknown
blinded the future
rupturing the vision
where the life boat
still waits.

Printed in the United States
By Bookmasters